Everything You Need To Know About

FAMILY VIOLENCE

Children want to feel safe with their families.

• THE NEED TO KNOW LIBRARY •

Everything You Need To Know About

FAMILY VIOLENCE

Evan Stark, Ph.D.

THE ROSEN PUBLISHING GROUP, INC.
NEW YORK

The people pictured in this book are only models; they, in no way, practice or endorse the activities illustrated. Captions serve only to explain the subjects of photographs and do not in any way imply a connection between the real-life models and the staged situations.

Published in 1989, 1991, 1993 by The Rosen Publishing Group, Inc.
29 East 21st Street, New York, New York 10010

Revised Edition 1993
Copyright 1989, 1991, 1993 by The Rosen Publishing Group, Inc.

Manufactured in the United States of America.

Library of Congress Cataloging-in-Publication Data

Stark, Evan
    Everything you need to know about family violence.
    (The need to know library)
    Bibliography: p. 62
    Includes index.
    Summary: Discusses facts about women and child
abuse and describes what victims of abuse are doing
to stop it.
    ISBN 0-8239-1755-X
    1. Family violence—United States—Juvenile literature.
[1. Family violence. 2. Child abuse. 3. Wife abuse] I. Title.
II. Title: Family violence. III. Series.
HQ809.3.U5878 1988
362.8'1   88-30739

Contents

Introduction

Roy Rowe did not celebrate his 17th birthday partying with his friends. He stood on his front porch, waiting for his stepfather to get home from work. When at last the man walked up the steps, Roy shot him—dead.

Why? Roy was a victim of child abuse. So were his younger sister and brother. Roy's mother was a victim of woman abuse. Many times their neighbors had called the police to report the screams coming from Roy's home. The stepfather was beating someone in the family with a paddle, a belt, or a two-by-four.

The children's teachers suspected child abuse and reported it. Relatives tried to help. But no one was able to stop the violence.

"I spent my whole childhood trying to get help," Roy later testified. "None ever came." That is why, on his 17th birthday, the boy killed his stepfather. For his crime, Roy was sentenced to four to twelve years in jail.

Roy and his family were victims of the two most common types of family violence: woman abuse and child abuse. Every year, about 4 million women in the United States are abused by their husbands or boyfriends. In fact, more women are injured by abuse than by auto accidents, rapes, and muggings combined.

Every 47 seconds, a child is abused or neglected in the United States. In one recent year, 2.7 million children and teenagers were physically, mentally, or sexually abused by family members.

But women and children are not always the victims. Husbands and fathers are not always the abusers. Many elderly people are also abused by those who are supposed to be taking care of them. Children are abused by day-care workers. Sometimes women abuse their husbands or boyfriends, not always physically but mentally.

Why do people hurt those they are supposed to love or care for? Who are the abusers? Where can victims like Roy and his family go for help? What can we do to stop family violence? This book will try to answer these and other questions about violence in American homes.

Anger and stress may lead to family violence.

Chapter 1

Abuse: What Is It? Who Suffers? And Why?

Upset by a long-distance phone bill, a father rams a gun into his teenage son's mouth and threatens, "Next time, I'll blow your brains out." A boyfriend, angry because his woman has moved out of their violent home, tricks one of her children into giving him her new address. The man goes to her home and breaks down the front door. He pushes his girlfriend against the cupboards, breaks her nose and ribs, and gives her two black eyes.

What Causes Abuse?

Many situations can lead to family violence.

• *Unreal expectations.* A mother may expect her son to do things he's not old enough to do. A three-year-old is probably too young to ride a two-wheel bike. When the child tries to ride and falls, the mother is angry. So she hits the child. This is abuse.

• *Stress.* A man may have had a bad day at work. There was a problem he couldn't solve, and his boss got angry. He feels put down and hurt. His wife has to work late. So she stops off and buys a frozen dinner. The man doesn't like frozen food. They argue. He throws the food at her. "I'll show you who's boss," he yells. This is abuse.

• *Emotional problems.* Some abusers were beaten as children. Others saw their parents use violence. Some abusers are uncomfortable with feelings like sadness, embarrassment, hurt, or even love. When they have these feelings, they get angry. They don't know how to use words.

• *Drinking or mental illness.* Some abusers are drunk. Some are jealous. Some are mentally ill. Some feel overwhelmed by problems. Some are just mean.

How Does Family Violence Start?

One thing all forms of family violence share is how they start. A desire to have control leads to the violence. The mother wants her son to ride a bike even though he is too young. Many thoughts go through her head. She thinks, "I will make him do it." Or she thinks, "I will teach him not to dis- obey me." She also thinks, "He is not riding the bike because he doesn't love me." She hits her son, and the boy keeps crying. Now she feels that things are really out of control. So she gets violent. The husband wants his wife to make up for his bad day. He feels, "I can't control what my boss does to me. But I can control her." Abusers use violence to control people who trust them.

All parents want their children to do the right thing. So when a child doesn't eat or dress properly, a mother or father may be upset, even mad. But an abuser doesn't need a reason to be mad or to hit. When an abuser gets violent, it is because of something that he or she sees, feels, or thinks. It is never because of something the child does.

What Is Abuse?

Abuse can cover a whole range of behaviors:

- *Physical abuse*—slapping, hitting, beating, or using weapons to hurt someone.
- *Verbal and emotional abuse*—when someone is constantly insulted and made to feel sad and worthless.
- *Rape and sexual abuse*—when one adult forces another adult or a child to have sexual intercourse or do other sexual things against their will, that is sexual abuse.
- *Total control*—one adult makes all the decisions for another person or for a whole family.
- *Neglect*—failure to provide proper food, clothing, medical care, supervision, and love.

Mental Abuse

Violence is only one method abusers use to get their way. They also threaten. They also deprive people of things they need to live, like money or food. Child abusers may lock children in the house during the day with no one to watch or feed them. A woman abuser may take his wife's money and pull out the phone.

Sixteen-year-old Shelby was a victim of mental abuse. The girl had worked hard to get the lead in her school play. She was very excited. At supper on opening night, Shelby was very nervous. She had no appetite. From across the table, her mother and stepfather glared at her. Shelby tried to explain that she had the jitters and just couldn't eat. But her mother said the food had been cooked and it must be eaten.

When Shelby protested, her mother got up and called the drama coach. She told him that her daughter would not be in the play. The coach was very upset. He tried to explain that this would ruin the play for the whole school and the rest of the parents as well. It made no difference. Shelby's mother was firm. She insisted that her daughter needed to be punished.

Shelby went to her room. She felt like killing herself. This could have been the best night of her life. Instead, it was the worst. But she was getting used to that. For years, her mother and stepfather had abused her mentally. They had done many things to make her feel worthless, embarrassed, and frustrated. So far, they had not hit her. But she often felt real pain just the same.

The Different Kinds of Abuse

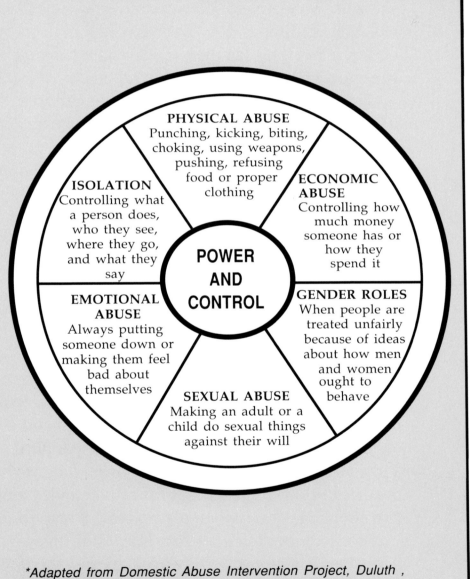

Adapted from Domestic Abuse Intervention Project, Duluth, Minnesota

Help for Abused Children

Once, not so long ago, if a child was beaten all the time, running away from home was the only way out. Many teens still run away to escape from violence. But today help is available for abused children and their families. Every state has services to protect children who are abused.

There are stories in this book about children who have been hurt by abuse. These children got help. Some were protected by the state. Some went to shelters. Some talked to teachers or other adults who would listen, believe them, and keep them safe. All of the stories in this book are true. These children still remember how hurt and afraid they were. But they were also brave. Today they live in homes where there is no violence. Once they were victims. Now they are survivors.

Help for Battered Women

At one time, if a woman was abused there were few places she could go for safety. Today, there are over 1,000 shelters in this country. Women and children can stay in a shelter until they feel safe and strong enough to live on their own. Later in this book you will read about Erin Pizzey and Sharon Rice Vaughan. These women started the first shelters.

Today family violence is a crime. This means that a family member can go to jail for deliberately hurting another family member.

Women Are Sometimes Abusers

The arguments between Shane and Laura had been getting worse for weeks. Shane tried to tell himself that his wife was under stress. But lately it seemed like she was just spoiled and unreasonable. Things always had to go her way.

One night when he came home late from work, Shane found all the locks on his house had been changed. When he called Laura from a friend's house, she told him to stay away from her and from David, their 8-year-old son. Shane loved his son. How could he live without seeing him?

Shane had never hit Laura. She had never hit him. But her mental abuse was making Shane very angry. He worried that her repeated mental abuse might make him become violent.

All men do *not* abuse women. Most do not. However, most people who do commit crimes of family violence are men or boys. Many boys believe they must keep their real feelings locked inside and not share them. When feelings are locked up, they can build until they explode into violence.

Women can be violent, too. Mothers as well as fathers abuse and neglect children. Women hit men and sometimes other women. Still, studies show that the persons who become trapped and controlled by violence are most often women and children.

Setting limits and correcting behavior is part of discipline.

Chapter 2

Abuse or Argument: Telling the Difference

This chapter shows the difference between discipline, fighting, and abuse.

Is It Discipline or Abuse?

Billy is supposed to be doing homework. But he's watching TV instead. His mother catches him and sends him to his room. He doesn't want to go. So she yells, "If you don't go now, you'll stay in your room till supper."

Imagine wrestling with your little sister. She hits her head and starts crying hard. Your father rushes in. He pulls you off and spanks your bottom. It makes you cry. But in a little while you forget it.

These are examples of discipline. The purpose of *discipline* is to correct behavior. It may be unfair to blame you when your sister gets hurt. You may feel that your father always takes your sister's side. Deep inside, though, you know he's trying to do what is right. He is trying to keep your sister safe.

Now think about this true story.

John couldn't read well. One day his father brought home *Big Red*, a book about a dog. John's father sat him in a chair and told him, "Read this." John tried, but he couldn't. He saw his father was getting angry. John was scared. "Read this," his father shouted again. Then he slapped John. John began crying. He had so many tears, he couldn't see the pages. But his father kept shouting, "Read this." His father slapped John many times.

This is *child abuse*. John can't read well. He will not learn to read if he is hit. John's father is hitting him because he doesn't know what to do with his own feelings. He is not angry because of anything John is doing. John's father feels ashamed that his son can't read well. He blames John for making him feel ashamed. How do you think John feels because he can't read well? Instead of trying to understand John's feelings and help him to read, his father beats him.

Now think about the following example.

Imagine that a little girl is hitting another girl over the head with a toy. What would be good discipline? What would be abuse?

One parent takes the toy away, saying that the child cannot play with it if she is going to hit another child. That is *discipline*.

Another parent breaks or throws away all the child's toys. That is *abuse*.

Is It Fighting or Abuse?

Family violence may start with an argument or even a fight. But it goes way beyond fighting.

Here are examples of fighting and abuse:

Peter's mother and her boyfriend disagree about whether she should work at night. He gets so mad that he yells at her and then walks out of the house.

"I'll be back in an hour," he says.

Later when he returns, the couple decides to hire a babysitter once a week so the two of them can spend time alone together.

This is *fighting*. Her boyfriend wanted Peter's mother to be home at night so they could be together. But he also respected her right to work at night. He knew she liked to work nights so she could be home when Peter returned from school. First her boyfriend was disappointed. Then he got mad because he didn't know what to say. So he walked out of the house. He admitted he was confused. He needed time to think things over.

When Jessica's father yells, she knows what will happen next. One night her mother had to work late. Her father was waiting up. There was good food in the refrigerator. All he had to do was heat it. But he decided not to eat. He just got madder and madder. When Jessica's mother returned, he grabbed her by the hair. Then he hit her in the face. "You won't do that again, you fat pig," he said. "I want you here to cook and clean. If you come home late again, I'll hurt you bad." Jessica heard her mom crying. The next morning, her father said he was sorry.

This is *abuse*. Jessica's father wants his wife home at night. But he does not respect her rights. He missed his dinner. Then he made himself mad about being hungry. He was confused. But instead of trying to get his feelings clear, he hid his feelings behind anger.

Abuse Rarely Happens Just Once.

Experts say that people who suffer abuse for a long time can feel it coming before it happens. They know what kinds of fights and arguments lead to abuse. They know the signs of violence, and watch for them. Even though outsiders may not see the signs, victims can tell when abusers are going to hurt them. They know because they have been hurt before.

Violence is not a one-time act. It is a cycle, a pattern. Unfortunately, abused children often turn into abusers themselves. The only way to stop the cycle is for victims and abusers both to get help.

Chapter 3

Behind Closed Doors

This chapter answers six commonly asked questions about family violence.

Question 1. *Some people say that what happens in your house is private. Are they right?*

No. Once a home was considered a man's "castle." The law paid no attention if he beat his wife or child. In fact, a man could use a stick, as long as it was no bigger around than his thumb. This was called "the rule of thumb." Children worked for their parents. It was common for a mother or father to beat children severely to make them obey. Boys and girls were raised to believe that what happened in their family was nobody else's business. Abuse was kept behind closed doors.

During the last century many groups fought against cruelty to children and women. Women demanded, and won, many rights. The law now protects children against having to go to work at very young ages. People have the right to privacy. But people also have the right to safety in their home, including women and children. Along with rights go responsibilities. We no longer believe that parents can abuse their own children. Parents are important people. But so are children. That's why we have laws against abuse.

Question 2. *Is family violence common?*

Some people claim that abuse is exaggerated. They think it is not really very serious. This makes people who are abused feel alone. They feel that what is happening in their lives is not happening to anyone else. So it is hard for them to tell anyone.

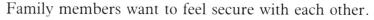

Family members want to feel secure with each other.

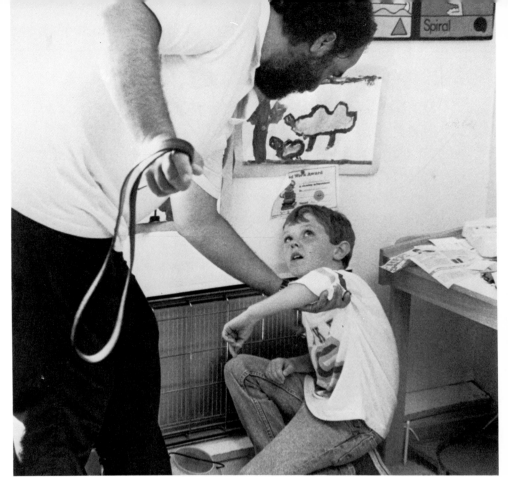

A child should not have to fear being hurt by adults, especially at home.

Unfortunately, abuse is more common than most people believe. Here are the facts:

• About 4 million women in the United States are abused every year by their husbands or boyfriends.

• More than 2.7 million American children (boys and girls) are physically, emotionally, or sexually abused by their parents each year.

• Abuse injures more women each year than any other single cause, even more than automobile accidents.

Question 3. *Does family violence happen only at home?*

Much of the time, it does. But abuse can happen in other places, too. When social workers went to the Harris home to check a report of child abuse, they found they were at the wrong place. The Harris's two pre-school children had been abused, not by their parents, but by the sitter at their day-care center.

Nearly 42 out of every 1,000 children in this country are abused in some way. Usually the abusers are parents or stepparents. But the violence doesn't always happen at the child's home. Many children are abused in day-care centers. Others are hurt by their mother's boyfriend or an aunt or uncle who is supposed to be caring for them. Often this abuse is sexual.

Violence also happens at institutions such as mental health centers and nursing homes. Elderly people or handicapped adults are often the victims. The abuse may be mental—a worker screaming insults at a patient. Or it can be physical—a worker may tie a patient into a chair for a long time for no reason. The patient may be neglected—have food or water withheld for long periods of time.

Workers are not the only abusers in institutions. Family members may neglect the patient by never going to see him or her. If they do go, they may hit or mentally abuse the patient by saying unkind things.

Abusers Come from All Walks of Life.

Abusers can be doctors or lawyers as well as workers in factories or stores. They come from all racial groups. They can be drunk or sober. Most abusers have no mental illness. Most abusers were abused themselves at one time. And yet there are many people who were abused as children who grow up to become warm and loving adults.

When people use violence in the family, it is usually because they think it will help them to get something they want. Some abusers use violence because they don't know how to get what they want in any other way. A single mother may turn to her child with needs that can only be met by another adult. When the child can't meet these needs, the mother gets abusive. A man may want to be comforted. But he may not know how to ask his wife to comfort him. He blames her for his failure, and he gets violent.

Question 4. *What is the relationship between woman abuse and child abuse?*

Most of the time, child abuse and woman abuse do not occur together. However, in almost half of all homes where there are abused children, the mother is also abused.

One common belief is that when a husband hits his wife, she will then beat her children. Sometimes this is true. Mothers are responsible for about 30 percent of all child abuse. Women do most of the parenting in our society. When children

Children are hurt by seeing parental violence.

are deprived of what they need to live, mothers are usually responsible. But men commit most of the physical abuse, particularly when severe injury to children is involved. The father or boyfriend in a family like this uses violence to control both the mother and the children.

Children can be hurt simply by seeing parental violence. Children who live in violent homes may wet the bed. They may do poorly in school. They may hurt their pets, or withdraw from their friends and keep to themselves.

Question 5. *How do abused people feel?*

An abused child feels like a hostage. She or he feels afraid, alone, and trapped.

When children are abused, if someone comes to help them, they may cling to the person who is hurting them. This is sad to see. These children do not like being hurt. But they want and need attention and love from their parents. They think the parent who is hitting them doesn't love them. They think they are hit because they are bad. So they cling.

Abused women may also feel trapped. They may lack money or a safe place to go. They don't want to leave their children. Or, like Jessica and her mom, they may be afraid to leave because they think the abuser will find them and hurt them worse. Jessica felt powerless. She wanted to help her mother. She was angry at her father, but was also afraid of him.

An abused person is usually insulted and "put down" as well as hit. Jessica's mom had been trying to lose weight. When Jessica's father called her mother "a fat pig," she felt terrible about herself. Abused children are often told they are "bad" or "no good."

Question 6. *What can abused women and children do?*

Today child abuse is a crime. Professionals and other adults must report abuse to a Child Welfare Service or to the police. Some of these services are listed at the end of the book.

Today we know that there are many nonviolent ways to discipline children or to disagree with adults. Violence is a choice people make. Only they are responsible for this choice. Nothing a child or an adult victim does causes abuse. And there is little a child can do to stop or prevent abuse. That is why we have services to protect and support victims.

When child abuse is reported, a child worker looks into it. If there is serious danger, the child is removed from the home and placed with another family to be safe. When the child is no longer in danger, the child worker can help the family learn how to deal with its problems in a better way.

In the last century, divorce for a woman was very hard. And it was very expensive. If a woman left a man, he got custody of the children, even if he was violent. Professionals did nothing about family violence. The police would not arrest a violent husband or parent. Doctors either ignored the problem or said it was the woman's fault. There was no safe place for abused women or children to go. They were trapped.

Things today are very different. Many women have good jobs. This means they can afford to live on their own. Many other women and children are supported by Aid to Families with Dependent Children (AFDC). Many women prefer to receive welfare, even if it makes them poor, than to live with a violent husband. Today women can go to court if they want a divorce, even if they are poor. In many parts of the country, police must arrest a person who has committed abuse. If a woman tells a judge she or her child is being beaten, the judge will give her a court order protecting her from the abuser. This is called "an order of protection."

During the 1980s, over 1,000 shelters for abused women and their children were opened all across the United States. Since that time, many more have opened. Men are not allowed to see their family members who are living in these shelters. Here, the women and children are safe.

In the shelters other abused women help each family to start a new life. The women and children learn that abuse is not their fault. They learn about equal rights. The shelters help women find jobs and safe places to live. The children learn to solve problems in ways that are not violent.

The first shelter for battered women was Chiswick House. It opened in 1971.

Chapter 4

The First Shelter: Chiswick House

Erin Pizzey is a very large woman with a loud laugh. She was born in China. During World War II, when she was only three years old, Erin Pizzey was captured by the Japanese. Sometime later she was exchanged for some other prisoners.

A Safe Place for Victims

When she grew up, Erin Pizzey lived in London, England. In the neighborhood where she lived there were many poor women. These women had no place to go where they could talk about their problems and just hang out. So Erin Pizzey found a house that was empty and free. Pretty soon the house was filled with women and children. Many of the women were being beaten by their husbands or boyfriends. The women felt like prisoners, a feeling that Erin Pizzey understood.

Erin Pizzey let the women stay in the new house. Some had been rich. Others had been poor. Some were Irish. Others were from as far away as India and Pakistan. The women left every-thing behind when they came to the shelter. The house became crowded and noisy. Sometimes two or three families slept in the same room. But the people who came were happy, because they were no longer prisoners.

There was a brick wall outside the house. One day the women painted a sign on the wall, "THIS IS A HOUSE FOR ALL WOMEN." This was Chiswick House, the first shelter in the world for abused women. It opened in 1971.

Chiswick House was always crowded. One night 30 women and children took some portable toilets and an old bus and drove to another part of town. There they found an old and empty hotel. They moved in, put up wallpaper, and opened an-other shelter. Today there are more than 100 shelters in England.

One day a man came to the front door of Chiswick House with a gun. Erin Pizzey opened the door and stood in front of him. She reached out for the gun, not knowing what the man would do. The man gave her the gun. She put her big arms around the man, and he started to cry.

Soon other men came to Chiswick House. At first they were angry. They blamed their violence on their wives and children. They said, "She made me do it." With Erin Pizzey's help, the men soon understood that violence was their problem. They began to talk about how to stop it. Today there are many groups for men who want to stop hurting the people they love.

Many teenage boys came to Chiswick House with their mothers. Some of these boys had been abused and were angry. Others were violent, even against their mothers. Erin Pizzey built a small house in the back where the boys could stay together. After school the boys helped out in Chiswick House. They used their money to buy motor-scooters. They met with a man who helped them understand why they were violent. The boys learned to argue without being violent. When they felt better about themselves, they treated others in a better way.

The story of Chiswick House illustrates several important points.

Abused women and children are strong and brave.

When people are being hurt by violence and insults, we call them victims. We may pity them. Remember, living with violence is not easy. Victims are always afraid and isolated. Some victims are put down so often that they no longer think clearly. They begin to believe that the abuse is somehow their fault. They think they are the only ones who are abused. They feel powerless.

If you feel like a prisoner, it takes great courage to escape. When abused women or children go for help, they are no longer victims. They are survivors. And they don't want pity.

Violent men can change.

The man who came to Chiswick House with a gun was hurt and sad that his wife and children had left him. But he hid these feelings with anger. He cried when Erin Pizzey took his gun away and hugged him. He realized that anger was not his real feeling. When he met with other violent men, he learned that no one had forced him to be violent. He alone was responsible for his behavior.

He learned that no one has a right to control another person. He also learned names for feelings other than anger. He learned that he could get his needs met only if he talked about them. He still sometimes feels "I'm so mad, I could..." But now, when this happens, he explains his feelings to his wife and leaves the house. He returns when he is no longer angry. Then they talk things over. Leaving when you are angry and coming back later is called a "time out."

Children in violent homes can become violent too.

The boys who came to Chiswick House got into fights and sometimes attacked their mother. When their father hit their mother, they felt afraid and powerless.

Listening to music can help an angry person calm down.

The boys learned that they could love their father, and even want to be like him without imitating his violence. They saw that abuse makes every child feel powerless and afraid.

Today the boys can deal with anger without getting violent. One boy goes to his room, turns on the stereo, and puts on his earphones. Another shoots baskets. Another writes poems. Another draws skeletons. One boy locks himself in the bathroom and screams at the top of his lungs. Several boys just go off by themselves and don't do anything.

What do you do when you're really angry?

Family violence can not be kept secret.

Chapter 5

Sharon Rice Vaughan and Women's Advocates

Sharon Rice Vaughan lives in St. Paul, Minnesota. She has three children. She and some friends started a phone service to help women solve their problems. The group was called "Women's Advocates."

If women wanted health care, Women's Advocates could tell them where to go. But most women who called wanted a safe place to stay. They were being beaten by their husband or boyfriend. Often their children were also being beaten.

When a woman and her children were in real danger, Sharon Rice Vaughan took them into her small apartment. The women and children who came had no money and few clothes. They slept

Women and children can relax in a shelter where they can feel safe.

on the floor. Sharon's daughter Rachel was in first grade. She went to a school with children who were rich. One day she came home very confused.

"Are we rich or poor?" she asked her mother.

She and her family had very little compared to the children in her school. But compared to the children who had been abused and who slept on the floor in her apartment, Rachel felt rich.

Soon the apartment was always crowded. Sharon Rice Vaughan decided to start a shelter like Chiswick House. She found a large home with five bedrooms. Then she and the others in Women's Advocates opened the first shelter in the United States for battered women.

The new shelter was quickly filled. But there were still problems. One night an angry man

broke the windows and scared the children. Another man broke into the house.

Day care was another problem. When the
abused women went to find a job or a place to live,
they could not take their children. So several men
volunteered to help with the children. Some
women were afraid to have men in the shelter. The
men they had known best were violent. But these
men were gentle and kind to the children.

When a woman first came to the shelter, she
told her story to the other abused women who
were already living there. Everyone tried to help a
newcomer as much as possible until she felt safe
and strong. The children in the shelter also had
tremendous needs. They played and went to
school with other children. But they felt different,
and they were ashamed because of the violence in
their lives. One day, Sharon had an idea. She put
the children on the radio to tell their stories.
People from all over the country heard what it was
like to grow up in a violent home. The program
won a national award. When this happened the
children felt good about themselves. They realized
that being different is not always bad. They were
proud to be survivors.

Help for the Women and Children

The shelter's biggest problem was money. The
women needed $24,000 to pay off a bank loan. If
they didn't get the money, they would lose the

house. Suddenly, as if by magic, hundreds of letters came from all over. The letters were from women and children who had heard about the shelter or had stayed there. The letters contained money. Most of the letters had only a few dollars inside. The money came from families on welfare as well as from rich women. The shelter survived on these pledges.

There are now more than 1,000 shelters for battered women in the United States.

The story of Sharon Rice Vaughan illustrates several points.

Listening and caring for people who are abused can make a big difference.

In the violent home, abused women and children are afraid and alone. They feel bad about themselves. In a shelter, abused women and children make all the decisions. They cook for one another, help one another find jobs and places to live. They learn that no one has a right to hurt them, even if they make mistakes. When they can control their lives in the shelter, they are ready to live on their own.

Not all men are violent.

When the shelter needed people to help with day care, several men volunteered. They built a play room in the basement. When the children watched these men, they saw how gentle and kind they were. These men sometimes got angry. But

when they did, they said what they felt. If they got
really mad, they turned around and walked away.
One man even made a joke out of his angry feelings, stamping around the room and bellowing like
an elephant. These men didn't hit or insult or
threaten the children. They treated boys and girls
like individuals. They let the boys cry and the girls
play sports. The children learned that there were
many different ways to handle feelings. The men
who worked at the shelter became models for the
children.

Most men are gentle, caring, and protective of children.

A woman has the right to call for help if she needs protection in her home.

Chapter 6

There Ought to Be a Law

Because of Tracey Thurman's courage, today woman abuse is a crime.

Should Police Get Involved in a Family Fight?

Tracey Thurman separated from her husband, Buck. She was 23. She went to stay with friends. Buck came to the friend's house where Tracey was staying. He grabbed her by the throat and threatened her. The friends called the police. But the police did nothing. The police believed that they had no right to interfere in this "private" fight. They thought that it was okay for Buck to hurt Tracey because he was her husband.

A few weeks later Buck came to the same house and took his two-year-old son by force. He is a huge man. He threatened to kill Tracey and the boy. This time he was arrested, but the charges were dropped.

A few days later Tracey was in her car. Buck came up to the car and started banging on the windshield. Finally, he smashed the windshield with his hand. A police officer who was watching did nothing. A court ordered Buck to stay away from Tracey, but Buck paid no attention.

The next month Buck threatened Tracey again. He did it again a month after that. Finally Tracey asked for a divorce. Then Buck said he would kill her and the boy. Once he tried to break into her apartment. Tracey told the police again, but they did nothing. They pretended they couldn't find Buck. So she told the police where he was staying.

Isn't Family Violence Against the Law?

Tracey was at a friend's house when Buck came to the door. He demanded that she talk to him. He had beaten her in the past. And he had threatened to kill her. So she called the police. She still hoped they might protect her.

When the police didn't come, Tracey went out. She wanted to persuade Buck not to hurt their son. Then a police car arrived.

Buck became violent. Suddenly he pulled a knife out of his pocket. He chased Tracey into the backyard. He grabbed her from behind, turned her around, and began stabbing her. Although the

Violence against others cannot be ignored.

police officer took Buck's knife, he did not arrest
Buck. While the officer and the little boy watched,
Buck returned to where Tracey was lying. He
kicked her many times in the head. More police
came. But Buck was still not arrested.

Tracey Thurman was in a coma for eight days
after the attack. She spent eight months in the
hospital.

Then Tracey got a lawyer and sued the police.
She charged that they should have arrested Buck
and put him in jail. They would have arrested him
if he had attacked someone on the street. Tracey
insisted that women deserve protection when they
are hurt by someone they know. It is the same as
when the are attacked by a stranger.

A Legal Victory for Battered Women

This was the first time a battered woman had
sued the police to get protection. Tracey had been
badly hurt. She was afraid Buck might kill her and
her son. But she stood up and bravely told what
had happened to her. Thousands of other women
have also told their stories.

Tracey won. The jury gave her 2 million dollars.
Then the state passed a new law. Now the police in
that state and in many other states must arrest a
man who hurts his wife or girlfriend.

Now family violence is a crime. No one has the
right to deliberately hurt another person, whether
they are married to that person or not.

What We Can Learn

The story of Tracey Thurman illustrates several things.

• *Family violence is not private.* Buck believed he could hurt Tracey and his son anytime he wanted to. The police believed this, too. No one has the right to hurt another person, no matter how much something bothers them. Today police must arrest someone who is abusive. Calling the police is a good way to keep someone from being abused.

• *Abuse rarely happens just once.* In most cases, when abuse occurs once, it will occur again. Some abusers are sorry for the violence and promise never to be violent again. But as soon as problems start at home, tension builds. Then the abuser gets violent again. This is called "the cycle of violence." Family violence stops only if the victim leaves and is safe, or something else is done to make the abuser change. Tracey's abuse only stopped when Buck was arrested and put in jail.

• *Most abusers are not sick.* Buck was not drinking when he stabbed and kicked Tracey. He was not on drugs. He was not mentally ill. He was just trying to control Tracey's behavior and get out his rage.

• *Men who abuse women often abuse children, too.* Buck took his son by force and threatened to kill him. This is child abuse. Half of all child abuse occurs when there is also woman abuse.

Violence affects not only the body but the mind as well.

Chapter 7

Inside a Violent Home

This is the true story of Audrey. She told the story when she went to a shelter for abused women. Audrey is 11. As you read her story, try to imagine what she is feeling.

Audrey's Story

I am here because my father batters my mom. My father is very cruel. He doesn't buy us any clothes. So we can't go to any parties. He won't even let my mother go out of the house. When we need something, we have to beg him for money. Whenever my father picks on my mother, I get nervous. I can't sleep, and sometimes I get very sick.

One Sunday evening my mother was combing my sister's hair. My dad picked up a big chair and he threw it. It hit my sister. It was meant for my mother. Every Sunday he picks on my mother. He won't even let her go to church.

Audrey's story illustrates several important points.

Abusers want control.

Audrey's father controls her by not letting her have any clothes. He controls his wife by not letting her go out, even to church. She has to beg him for money. These are all forms of abuse.

This kind of control isolates the person who is being abused. The children had no clothes, so they couldn't go to parties. Audrey's mother could not go out of the house, even when her father was not at home. Audrey's mother was afraid he would find out, and hit her. When people are isolated this way, they get no support. They can't tell anyone what is happening to them. They think the abuser has all the power in the world. They are too scared to leave.

Victims are made dependent.

Audrey's father wouldn't let her mother have any money. Her mother was completely dependent on him for survival. Audrey had no allowance. She and her mother had to beg her father for anything they wanted. By controlling their money, Audrey's father could make them behave the way he thought women should. He could be "boss."

Audrey's mother was very religious. She had been going to church every Sunday since she was little. When Audrey's father kept her from going to church, she realized how bad her situation really was. She had lost her independence. She no longer had the freedom to live the way she wanted. This man was deciding what she could or could not do. It was then that she stood up to her husband and went to the shelter.

Seeing family violence can make children sick.

Children may be hurt accidentally when their parents fight. When Audrey's father threw a chair at her mother, it hit her sister. But children are hurt the most inside. They get upset, and afraid. Audrey had trouble sleeping at night. Sometimes, when her parents were fighting, she got sick.

Sometimes when children see abuse, they have nightmares. Many have trouble sleeping. Little children often wet the bed. Sometimes older children wet the bed, too. Children may also have trouble in school. They may get into fights with their friends. Or they may retreat into silence and stop playing with their friends. Sometimes children who are abused take out their anger on pets, and may even kill them. Sometimes they become very passive and quiet and always seem sad. If you have friends that behave this way often, they may be abused.

Teenagers may feel the desire to protect the family from a violent parent or boyfriend.

Chapter 8

Family Violence Can Be Stopped

This is the story of 13-year-old Regina. Regina has gone with her mother to a shelter for abused women.

Regina's Story

I am here because every night when my dad said he was going out he kept saying, "Come on out for a drink." Mom said, "No, I'm staying home because I'm tired and want to go to bed." He would go out and get drunk. He would come back and beat up my mom with me watching and listening.

When he beat up my mom, my big brother would try to stop him. But my dad would push him away. So he would call someone like me to help him. But my dad would just shout at me to go away, and then push me, too.

One day I came in from school. When my dad saw my room he said, "Why haven't you cleaned up, you lazy cow?"

I tried to talk to him, but he wouldn't listen. I said to him, "You are supposed to clean up while Mom's at work." But he hit me and sent me to bed. He wouldn't let me come down for supper. Later, Mom brought me some potato chips. But he found out and beat my mom up again. I came here because my dad tried to strangle my mom and she couldn't stand it anymore, so we left.

Only the abuser can stop the violence.

Regina and her older brother tried to protect their mom when she was attacked. But even though they were both teenagers, their father pushed them aside. When this happened they felt that they had failed their mom. Her brother thought, "If I were a real man, I could protect my mother."

When Regina told her mom that she had been hit and had missed supper, her mother gave her some potato chips. When her father found out, he hit her mom. Regina felt this was her fault. If she had kept quiet, her father would not have been violent.

Sometimes even Regina's mother felt the violence was her fault. She thought, "Maybe if I went out drinking with him, he wouldn't hit me." But she was too tired after a long day at work.

No one in a family can stop the violence except the person who is abusive. Regina's father was abusive because of what he felt, not because of anything Regina, her brother, or her mother did.

Abused children feel trapped.

Abused children have confusing feelings. They feel trapped. They are also scared. They feel guilty. They think they may be responsible for the violence. They may also feel ashamed because this is happening to them. At the same time, many abused children feel loyal to their parents. They want and need attention and love, and they deserve it. When the person who is supposed to love them hurts them instead, they may feel it is because they are bad. Abusive parents are often very cold to their children. Some children want attention from their parents so badly that they confuse getting hit with getting attention. For all these reasons, children may not want to talk about abuse.

An abusive boyfriend.

Like other people, Pete and Tashica argued sometimes. Tashica took karate classes after school, and she liked to practice on Saturday mornings. Tashica was working on her brown belt.

One night after a movie Pete and Tashica were walking to get some ice cream. Three older boys approached, all bigger than Pete.

"Wanna come with us?" one of the boys asked Tashica.

"No way," she said.

The boys surrounded Tashica and Pete.

The one who had spoken first came up close to Tashica.

"You sure?" he asked.

Girls have a right to defend themselves.

Before she could answer, Pete pushed the boy.

"Let's teach him a lesson," the first boy said. They started hitting and kicking Pete, knocking him down.

Things were happening fast. With a quick move, Tashica hit the biggest boy in the stomach. He doubled over. Then she kicked the second boy hard in the shins. The boys were stunned. By the time Pete got to his feet, they had left.

The next day in school Pete was quiet. He didn't call Tashica that night or the next. She was worried. Had she done something wrong? Several days later, Tashica got a note to meet Pete after school. Pete was furious at her for fighting with the boys.

"I do my own fighting," Pete said. "You're my girl and I'll protect you."

Tashica explained that the boys were talking to her, not to him. She told him that she liked him. But she didn't need his protection. Tashica said this gently. But Pete got even angrier. He grabbed her arm tightly. "Let go," Tashica said. Suddenly, without warning, Pete pushed her hard to the ground. Then he walked off.

Sexism can lead to violence.

Pete made all the decisions for Tashica. At first Tashica thought this was cool. Pete was just like a "Prince Charming." He even opened doors for her. But Pete was angry about Tashica's karate lessons. Pete treated her like his property. He wanted to take care of her in his own way. Pete couldn't accept Tashica for who she was.

Some men feel that they are better than women—stronger, smarter, more able to handle problems. They think men should be the bosses of their women. This is *sexism*. These men have strict ideas about how women should behave. Men that think in sexist ways want to control women. Sexism can lead to family violence.

Stopping family violence means changing behavior.

Family violence can be stopped. But abusers must want it to stop. They must want to end their violent behavior. Here are some ways:

• *Admit anger.* Anger is a normal *emotion*. It helps a person to admit that he or she is angry, before the anger turns to violence. It's OK to say, "I'm upset with you. I'm getting angry. Let's talk about this before I lose my temper."

• *Learn to handle jealousy.* Feelings of jealousy often happen when one person tries to control another. Men must remember that they do not own their wives or girlfriends. Parents do not own their children. Jealousy also happens when a person does not feel good about himself or herself (poor self-esteem).

• *Listen to the other person.* When you are in an argument with a person, it's natural to think that you are right and he or she is wrong. But usually

both sides are at fault. Next time, instead of yelling
back, be quiet. Listen—*really* listen. Try honestly
to put yourself in the other person's place and see
the argument from his or her side.

 • *Reduce stress.* We live in a high-speed world.
There is pressure to work hard, to be successful, to
make money. This pressure causes stress, which
can lead to violent behavior. When you're under
stress, take a time-out. Listen to music. Take a
walk. Go to a room by yourself and do some deep
breathing. Close your eyes.

 • *Don't drink or use drugs.* Statistics show that
in 60 to 80 percent of family violence cases, one or
more people had used drugs or alcohol. Stopping
this use can help stop family violence.

 • *Be an optimist.* Think positively, no matter
how bad your situation may seem. People who
believe that life and people are basically good are
much less apt to be violent.

When you're the victim, speak out!

Victims can help stop family violence only by
speaking out. It is understandable if you are afraid,
but keeping quiet only helps the violence continue.

It takes great courage to speak out. Sometimes
your worst fears come true. Staying silent, however, does *not* solve the problem. Going to the
police, a shelter, or a counselor is the best way for
victims to stop family violence and take control of
their own lives.

Glossary—*Explaining New Words*

abuse The use of violence to control another person. Deliberately hurting someone you are supposed to care about or care for. The person who uses violence against another is the *abuser*.

battered Hit, beaten, abused.

custody The legal responsibility to protect and care for another person, usually a child.

cycle An action that happens over and over again.

discipline Training to develop good behavior. Sometimes punishments are used, but never violence.

emotional Having to do with strong feelings of the mind and heart.

expectations Goals, plans that a person is expected to achieve.

independence Freedom from being controlled by another.

institution A care center set up to serve people with special needs.

neglect Failure to take proper care of someone.

optimist One who looks on the bright or positive side of life.

prisoner A person forced to live without personal rights.

rape When one person forces another person to have sexual relations.

sexism Unfair comments or actions toward women which make them seem inferior to men.

shelter A safe space where victims of abuse and violence can recover from their hurt and injuries.

stress Force, pressure, or mental strain.

survivors Victims of abuse who have gotten help.

"time out" When someone who feels "I'm so angry I could..." stops and goes somewhere else to manage their feelings.

violence Use of strong physical force.

Where To Go For Help

LOCAL RESOURCES

School personnel
Police officers
Doctors
Members of the clergy
YWCAs
Battered Women's Shelter
Family and Children Services
Child Protective Services.

CHILD HELP USA
National Abuse Hotline
1-800-422-4453
(1-800-4-A-CHILD)

PARENTS ANONYMOUS
1-800-421-0353

NATIONAL COMMITTEE
FOR PREVENTION OF
CHILD ABUSE
332 South Michigan Ave
Chicago, IL 60604
(312) 663-3520

NATIONAL COALITION
AGAINST DOMESTIC
VIOLENCE
P.O. Box 18749
Denver, CO 80218-0749
(303) 839-1852

EMERGE: A MEN'S COUN-
SELING SERVICE ON
DOMESTIC VIOLENCE
18 Hurley St. Ste. 100
Cambridge, MA 02141
(617) 422-1550

For Further Reading

Johnson, Becca Cowan. *For Their Sake*. Martinsville, IN: American Camping Association, 1992, 204 pp. Discusses ways of recognizing, responding to, and reporting child abuse.

Landau, Elaine. *Child Abuse: An American Epidemic*. New York: Messner, 1984, 117 pp. Case histories of battered children are used to reveal the many forms abuse can take.

Licata, Renora. *Everything You Need to Know about Anger*. New York: The Rosen Publishing Group, Inc., 1992, 64 pp. A guide for students and their families to understand and deal with their angry feelings.

Pizzey, Erin. *Scream Quietly or the Neighbours Will Hear*. New York: Penguin Books, 1974, 143 pp. This book tells the story of Chiswick House, the first battered woman's shelter.

Toufexis, Anastasia. "When Kids Kill Abusive Parents," *Time*, November 23, 1992, pp. 60–61.

There is a book available from the Resource Center for the Prevention of Family Violence and Sexual Assault: *Preventing Family Violence*. This book uses case materials and classroom exercises to review issues of abuse. Write to the center listed above at 150 Tremont Street, Boston, MA 02111.

Index

About the Author
Evan Stark is a well-known sociologist, educator, and therapist—as well as a popular lecturer on women's and children's health issues. Dr. Stark was the Henry Rutgers Fellow at Rutgers University, and associate at the Institution for Social and Policy Studies at Yale University, and a Fulbright Fellow at the University of Essex. He is the author of many publications in the field of family relations and is the father of four children.

Acknowledgments and Photo Credits
Cover photo by Stuart Rabinowitz
Photograph on page 36: New Haven Project for Battered Women; photos on pages 30,38: Evan Stark; art on page 13: Blackbirch Graphics, Inc.; all other photos by Stuart Rabinowitz.

Design/Production: Blackbirch Graphics, Inc.